Revelations *of my* Heart

Poems, Prayers, Notes & Quotes

Kimberly E.M. Beasley

HunnyChild Books

DEDICATION

This book is dedicated to the Loves in my life.
For the Loves that has passed on and for the ones that
remain.

CONTENTS

ACKNOWLEDGMENTS

To my parents Frederick and Cheryl Maddox; My Pillars! Thank you for believing in me, praying for me and crying for me when I had no more tears. Thank you for teaching me the importance of God, Love, Family and Forgiveness.

To my "Sissy"…You have always been special to me and thank you for the unselfish sacrifice you made to be with me during some of my darkest hours. Your presence made the difference. You gave me hope and "Po-Lisad" me during my fight…LOL!

To my brother Freddie…Thank you for reminding me that I am beautiful, even when I didn't see it myself. Your faith, prayers, laughter and encouragement helped to dry my tears many days. You are an inspiration to me.

To my brother Jerry and sister Renee…Thank you for being confidants, encouragers and the voice of reason so many days. Thank you for sharing your wisdom, laughter and especially your shoulders. Your support and love is vital to me.

To my sons…What can I say…You are Courageous! You are Unique! You are Brilliant! I am so proud of you. God must have thought I was really special to bless me with you. You are remarkable young men, you are strong and I'm amazed at the wisdom you have displayed at such tender ages. You are my miracles!

To my husband…You make me better. You have inspired me in so many ways and have helped me to become better in so many areas of my life. Your love and faith in me has never wavered and I thank you for believing in me even when I doubted myself. You are a rare jewel; truly a remarkable man and I will cherish you forever!

Special Note

Family I can't say thank you enough. You are so special to me and want you to know that I am thankful for you. Thank you for riding through the storms with me. I don't know what the future holds but what I do know is that God is in complete control. I completed this book with all of you in mind. You have been strong for me so many days and I just want you to always know that no matter what comes your way, God is there. Trust in Him completely. Believe in Him wholeheartedly and stop believing the lies of the devil. I want you to know that I love you but God loves you best. Pursue righteousness; your life depends on it. I hope this book brings you joy every time you read it. You all have taught me how to truly do love. You gave me good practice and I love you for that. God has blessed me with you, and I hope I have been a blessing in return to you. Live each day as if it is your last, make peace whenever it is possible and love joyously everywhere you go. Oh, don't forget to laugh! Let it become part of your daily living. This is what I'm trying to do and this is how I want you to remember me. By…My…Love!

INTRODUCTION

So many times my husband has said that I should do something with my writing. He has been one of my biggest fans. I have always enjoyed writing and secretly wanted to write a book but truth be told I was really afraid of possible rejection. It wasn't until I was faced with some life altering events in 2013, I decided no longer will I be concerned about other people accepting me nor pleasing them any longer. A cancer diagnosis will definitely get you to reevaluate your life's purpose and mission. I realized that I had devoted many years to people pleasing and forgot all about me.

It was a bitter pill to swallow when I was diagnosed with cancer and all the people I thought would be there to support me weren't there. I realized that I expected them to respond how I would have responded had it been one of them battling a potentially fatal disease. I felt abandoned in more ways than one. My life was spiraling out of control and it was nothing I could do about it. I was wounded by some of those who claimed to have loved me so much. Instead of focusing on and picking those wounds; I opened my heart to forgiveness and the love that had been strategically placed around me. I noticed how prayers that I had prayed several years prior had been answered. I saw relationships that I desired being cultivated and some aspects of others end. I had no idea of the blessing that would come from what seemed to be such a disaster. God knew exactly what I needed at that time in order to comfort me and I found solace with my pad and pen. The pressures of life pushed me to pull out old journals of poetry and pressed me to push my pen. The outcome was "Revelations of my heart".

Love is the central theme in "Revelations Of My Heart.". It is an intimate collection of poems, prayers, notes and quotes. Every word was inspired by my life experiences, special people in my life and the love I withheld from myself. I've learned that the way I treat myself is the only way I really can treat others anything else is deceptive. I couldn't love my fellow man as myself because I withheld love from myself. I am no longer deceptive and I'm not ashamed or afraid of my truth. "Revelations of my heart" has given me courage to be who I am; Nothing more, nothing less. My experiences no longer define me, I have finally defined myself!

My desire is that you are able to visualize the passages that I've penned and find hope throughout the journey.

"God knew my tomorrow before my

yesterday
He's already visited my today
I'm just catching up to my tomorrow…today"

~Kimberly E. M. Beasley

"*L*OVE"

1 CORINTHIANS 13

Love – Agape: This is not based on passion; it's not a feeling. It's a commitment based on principle!

Verse 1:
If I can speak in a language that is understood by angels, possessing every imaginable mode of speech but don't love; My words are not lasting just as the sound from a cymbal or a gong piercing the ears of the hearers but only for a moment and then it vanishes quickly.

Verse 2:
Even if I have the gift of prophecy, which is a great gift to the church; or being able to reveal all mysteries and all scientific theories. If I have a faith that can tell a mountain get out of my way and it moves; but don't love...I am nothing.

Verse 3:
I can give everything I possess including the clothes off my back and give my body over to be burned as a martyr but don't love...
All that was done meant nothing and nor did I gain a thing. So no matter what I say, what I believe, what I do none of these things mean a thing without love.

Verse 4:
Love never gives up – It's patient, longsuffering
Love cares for others more than for self – It's kind
Love doesn't want what it doesn't have – It's not envious

or jealous

Love doesn't boast or brag – It doesn't parade itself

Love doesn't have a swelled head – It's not proud

Verse 5:

Love doesn't force itself on others – It's not rude or disrespectful

Love isn't me first, it's not about me, my wants, desires or feelings…It's about others – It's not self-seeking

Love doesn't fly off the handle, it is not quick tempered or huff and puff – It's not easily angered or provoked

Love doesn't keep score of the sins of others – It doesn't keep record of wrongs

Verse 6:

It does not enjoy doing or thinking wrong, wicked or sinful – It takes no pleasure in what is evil; it rejoices with the truth

Verse 7:

Love is a roof that covers and protects all that is under its shelter – It bears all things

Love always trust – in all things

Love always hopes – It always looks for the best

Love perseveres – it never looks back, it remains steadfast in the face of unpleasant circumstances

Verse 8:

Love never fails – Love is permanent and will never come to an end…It's eternal!

But prophecies…are not eternal. They will come to an end. As well as tongues, they will also end. All knowledge theoretical and scientific will reach its limit and meet its end. These things will be rendered obsolete. But not Love.

Verse 9:
Everything we know is only a portion of something greater. Even when we prophesy it's not complete.

Verse 10:
But when the end comes or appears what is known and prophesied will disappear.

Verse 11:
Look at it this way. When I was a child, an infant or immature, my language was that of an infant. I was simple minded and understood like a child would. My very thoughts were that of a child. When I grew up and became mature all that I did as a child, how I spoke, my level of understanding and my thought patterns were not the same. It became apparent that I was no longer a child and neither would ever be again.

Verse 12:
Right now we see things indirectly and imperfectly through a mirror where our reflection is total opposite of what our reality is. But then we will see face to face with total clarity. Right now all I know is partial and incomplete. But then I will know completely just as God already knows me now.

Verse 13:
But for now stand in the truthfulness of our God. This is our faith; stand in expectation of His glorious appearance. This is our hope. Stand in love. Make a deliberate choice

to love. These three things be steadfast in.
But above all our responsibilities to love is the greatest.

Summary of Love:

Love Is: Patient, Kind
Love Does Not: Envy, Boast, Keep record of wrongs,
Delight in evil
Love Is Not: Proud, Rude, Self-seeking, Easily angered
Love Does: Rejoice with truth, Protect, Always trusts,
Always hopes, Always perseveres
Love Never: Fail

I Must Begin With Loving Me

I will no longer reject myself and tell myself I'm not good enough. I will be patient with me, kind to me; I will no longer remind myself of my past failures and hold onto to self-anger and self-condemnation. I will pray for myself and rejoice freely when I accomplish what has been set for me to do. I will fight for me…I'm worth it!

I realize that I can't love anyone without genuinely and unconditionally loving myself. Of course when asked if I loved myself my answer was yes. But after carefully examining the way I have treated myself, it was far from it. The truth of the matter is if I was in a relationship with someone that treated me the way I have treated myself; I would have ended the relationship.

I used 1 Corinthians 13 as my love gauge. Based on that premise, I had failed at loving myself. It was a hard truth to accept, but nonetheless it was the truth. I was willing to take the first step at truly loving myself by accepting my truth. I realized that I had learned to neglect and sacrifice myself in what I call "In the name of love for others." But I had not learned how to unconditionally love myself.

The Bible teaches us to love our neighbor "As" our self, but how can we love our neighbor if we have a misconception of what loving our self is? It is impossible to love anyone further than what our own love of self is. Anything further than that is deceptive in nature and ritualistic. We have become accustomed to behaving in a manner in which is perceived to be patient and kind, etc.; an outward display of these attributes, but our hearts are not there. Take note of your inner dialog the next time you are at a gathering. You might or might not be surprised at the not so kind thoughts you are having that your actions aren't displaying.

I have made a vow to love myself no matter what. I have also vowed to stop people pleasing. Whenever I find myself reverting back to old patterns I quickly check it and weight it against my love gauge. Because I desire to love others genuinely and unconditionally; it is a must to master loving me.

Before I am... I was

9

How can I get back to that place where pain was lost and forgotten
And how could I desire freedom that has never been spoken of
Trying to remember that place
The very place I was
Beyond my mother's womb
A spirit from Self-existent himself
In that place was there time and space
Was there any darkness
In that place where I was
Were there suns, moons and stars
What about big bright cotton like clouds
That I enjoying seeing where I am
Where I was in that place
Was there joy, serenity, pure bliss
Was there a need to escape and just clear your mind
Or was the brilliance of beauty mind blowing at every glance
Was there a need for air, for water, for food
Or a place to rest my head
What about stress from trying to make ends meet
Like there is where I am
What about the second place where I was
Before I got to where I am
Not even a mere distant memory found in the recesses of my mind
No spark, no flame, none that I remember
When I was closest to my mother
I don't remember the flips or kicks

That were associated with the mystery of where I was
What about the hiccoughs that I used to get
Did I suck my thumb?
What did my father's voice sound like and my mother's
too
Was the rhythm of my mother's heartbeat the first music I
danced to
People say where I am…in that place where I was
You can open your eyes, feel and hear
Why is it all forgotten?
What did I see where I was
Inside my mother's womb
Did I leap for joy
When I saw her joy
Did my eyes cry
When I saw her pain
Did I cover my ears
When I heard every secret she thought she'd never speak
Did I fold under the pressure I was feeling
Desiring to go back to the first place I was
Cramped and consumed was I extremely confused
Feeling as though the walls have closed in on me…where
do I go from here
How do you escape from this type of pain.
I can't move
It's difficult to breathe
I was at the point of death
I am no longer dancing to the rhythm of my mother's
heartbeat
But somewhere in the silence I heard another rhythm
I think it's mine

After all this time dancing to someone else's beat
How do I ever begin to dance to my own
It seems where I am
I'm constantly getting off beat
Somehow ending up following someone else's
Doing their dance
As soon as I begun to dance
To the rhythm of my own beat
It seemed my music stopped
I was dancing…then she rejected me
I was dancing…then they touched me
I was dancing
When he said he didn't want me
I was dancing
When he liked me
This time I kept dancing until…
I let him…
Then he left me
I was dancing
Then sickness and failure came
I was trying to find my beat
When an undesired marriage came
Then abuse came
I was lost in this rhythm less tango
Filled with pain, fears, disappointment, secrets
Feelings I never uttered to a soul
Except the one that heard them
While dancing in my wounds
It seems where I am
There's no room for dancing
So I gave up on dancing to my tune
In order to preserve my sons

I was divorced and heard a little thump
Then I experienced a tremendous loss
A woman I saw dancing my entire life…my grandmother
The thump I was hearing slowly dissipated
Into the darkness of my despair
I was sick in my body
A single mother
A grief stricken grand-daughter
A battered ex-wife
Indulging in alcohol and other drugs
An embarrassed aunt
I was reckless…
An insufficient soldier
An insecure teen
A rejected sister
A confused daughter
A violated little girl
Now add i am
Surgically barren and a cancer patient
Why does it seem
For all the joy you get twice the pain
I wish I could go back
To the place
Where pain was lost and forgotten
But I can't go back
To where I was
Because I'm still here
All that I was
Is a part of who i am
A not so distant memory of
Where I used to be
Although I am not dancing yet

There is a new rhythm to my beat
Something that wasn't there before
At times it makes me sit and tap my feet
This rhythm sometimes fills my eyes with tears
When I hear secrets not spoken before
The pain that's in this melody
Is sometimes the pain it feels for me
This rhythm reminds me of somewhere I was
In an ever so distant past
It's warm, safe, ideal for me
I feel at home
Like this is where
I am supposed to be
But I still get lost
Trying to find my beat
I am stuck where I was
Longing to be where I am
I am a daughter, a sister, a niece, a cousin
I am an aunt, a mother, a wife and step-mother
I am a friend, a Christian, a pet owner
I am committing myself to be better than I was

The day will come
When I can stand in all truth and say
I was rejected…now I am loved
I was violated…now I am protected
I was confused…now I am understanding
I was insecure…now I am confident
I was victimized…now I am a fighter
I was in despair…now I am optimistic
I was embarrassed…now I am an honor
I was reckless…now I am responsible

I was insufficient…now I am able
I was a cancer patient…now I am a survivor
I was lost…now I am found
I am waiting to hear my rhythm
And dance to my own beat
It's been an experience dancing for others
I am ready to dance for me

My Mentors Of Love

17

God loved me so much…He blessed me to have my mother's love, my father's love, and the love of 4 wonderful grandparents. For that I am grateful!

Every person deserves to be loved. God loved us while we were in our own mess. The world will see us and know us by our love. Practice love so that it is perfected in you. Agape, not a feeling of passion but a commitment to a principle.

Grandpa

Thick hands and broad shoulders
The epitome of a strong man
Tough chin, solemn grin
Bold in stature, honest in deed
Milk chocolate skin
A stern disciplinarian
A man of integrity
This is what I remember Grandpa to be
Loving, kindness, tender and meek
With Sunday being his favorite day of the week
Giving and living 93 years
Without once letting us see him shedding tears
Oh what a man, to have in my life
Being married and committed to his only wife
Grandpa was devoted as you can see
The years he was married were 63
Not an egotist, proud or arrogant in demeanor
But cool, calm, and collected
Among everyone he was respected
Grandpa had profound silence
A man of few words
The hinges of his mouth was wisdom
And that's what he spoke
A deep baritone voice is how I remember it to be
And he sang melodious melodies
This is how I remember Grandpa to be
Peaceful, humble, studious, astute
Not to mention wear my looks came from
My Grandpa was quite cute

Handsome would be a more masculine word

The man many people loved to love
Underlying qualities, a blessing from God above
I'll always remember Grandpa like this
Honest, plain, simple unique
Content and free
A living example for me

Grandma

Broad hips and long hair
Caramel colored skin, slightly thick not too thin
Grandma was a sight for sore eyes
Full of integrity
No compromise
When she walked, you heard confidence in her feet
And oh so elegant, to those she would meet
Grandma was a lady many admired
Her hands worked art; her lips spoke words that inspired
She had a love so genuine and real
A strong woman is how I remember Grandma to be
And she had no problem saying her favorite was me
And I can't forget the times we've shared
When it was just me and her
The only ones there
The long talks in the middle of the night
Grandma saying it will be all right
Knowing just when to be right there
She had a special way to show she cared
She gave tender kisses and a joyous smile
And second nature to go the extra mile
Having no worries or any cares
For she knew God was always there
A Grandma that words can't define
And I'm glad to say that Grandma is mine

Daddy and Momma

It was the month of June year 1973
The month and year my momma gave birth to me
My daddy said it was the hottest day of the year
But that didn't stop him from being right there
I was the youngest born to them
Out of three
Lisa, Frederick Jr. and Kimberly
Daddy and Momma have been married for several years
They've shared joy, pain, hysterical laughs and copious
tears
I have had the pleasure of watching them from afar
They thought no one was looking while they kissed in the
car
Momma would blush when daddy called her cute names
Daddy would pop his collar when she did the same
They sometimes took bike rides together
Under the stars and moon
Or slow danced while daddy serenaded momma
One of her favorite tunes
I know all hasn't been easy
They might not have gotten everything right
But they stuck in there together and are still in the fight
They've watched other couples give up and walk out
I'm sure they've thought of letting go too without a doubt
Daddy and Momma taught me something
About marriage and love
No matter the circumstances you are faced with
Together you can rise above

You

I look in your eyes, ever so bright
Falling in love again
It grows ever so deeply
Love fills my heart with every pound
Taking my breath away, my heart begins to race
What would life be without you
I prayed that one day I would have you a part of my life
I prayed for you and you chose me
I want to be all I can be for you
Depriving you of nothing
And asking you for nothing in return
For I know as long as I do what I'm supposed to do
I'll receive my just reward
As we grow older, we grow closer
I fall deeper in love and hoping that I have fulfilled all I
was to do
And teaching you all a single mother could teach her son

GOD CREATED ME FROM YOU FOR YOU

We talked for hours last night about our relationship and where we wanted to be in regards to loving one another. We realized a long time ago that we were created to be together. God is truly faithful and loves me so much that He led me to this gift of a man. It wasn't good for him be alone so he created an opposite counterpart for him...me. When the Lord brought me to this man he replied "This woman is bone of my bones and flesh of my flesh." He said I was the BOMB! I am "The BOMB!" This love is explosive! ...One Rib, One Woman!

One

All at once my life has changed
Nothing inside of my world could ever be the same
All of my days
I've waited subconsciously for this very moment
When my soul, my heart, the very breath I breathe
Would be in unison with you
The pulse of my destiny
Is beating once again
The vision of my purpose is no longer dim
The purpose of my existence
The essence of my being
Is in perfect harmony with the flesh of your heart
The sound of each pounding moment
Like the rushing of blood through the veins
One mind, one heart, one body, one soul
One man, one woman and the two
Became One…

"God put a stamp on our intimate passion. I rejoice in the sensuous pleasures of my husband's kisses and he is wholly desirable to me. Thank you Lord for showing me that he is to be my best friend, and more than a friend...He is my lover!"

*L*ove…My Love…

⧓

Like an apple tree among the trees in the forest. So are you my Love among men. I delight to sit in your shade and your fruit is sweet to my taste. Song of Songs 2:3 (personalized)

These words aren't for flattery. I'm simple making an attempt to pen my heart on this piece of processed wood. I know I've told you many times before how much I love and care for you. This is not one of those times. I know I've told you how much I appreciate you, but again this is not one of those times. It is not because I don't love and care for you. Nor is it because I don't appreciate you, this time I wanted to let you know why and how much I respect you as my husband, my lover, my friend and for the father you are to our children.

I respect you for the man you are and the man you are striving to be. I see the diligence in your pursuit to do what is pleasing to God concerning us. Although you may feel at times you are not doing enough in the kid's lives, but I beg to differ. Our children have a living example in you of what a responsible and honorable man is. You use your God given ability and strength to work in order to provide for the family. You protect us with your God given wisdom and guide us even from afar. Your voice is heard and your spirit is ever present. There is not a day that goes by we're not looking to follow your lead. Believe it or not; whatever you say really does go. We are blessed of God to have a man in our lives such as you.

I respect you for the sacrifices you have made for me. As I think about how your love has been so sacrificial, I can't help but to thank God for the courage you have to love me the way you do. I love the way you love me. The Bible

49

says that "God is Love", your very name means "God like". The way I see it, you're named "love". God equipped you to share your gift of love with me. There is no way you can do love except it be by the Spirit of God. Yes, I said do love. With me you have been patient, kind and humble. You have not been rude, proud, selfish nor were you easily angered. You are not jealous and you don't hold grudges. You love the truth and don't pursue to do evil.

You are protective; you give me hope that preserves me. Your love is successful. Not many people have what I have in a man. You have accomplished a great task. Not that it has been mastered; but it is truly in operation and maturing.

This is what makes you an apple tree in a forest of evergreens. Undoubtedly, this is what sets you apart from all other men; in your workplace and the community. I know this is why others admire you, because of the way you do love...

You are like "Love". I will no longer question or doubt your love for me. I see it clearly. I respect your passion in love and your commitment to love. This gives me security and ecstasy knowing your devotion to me. I am committed to our love being done...You inspired me!

God is Love and like Love is You...

"I developed a mindset of intimate passion. I think about my beloved and my desire toward him. My mind is made up…I'm in a mood for love. I serve him with my body and my body adores him. I cherish his body and declare its worth with my body. I give myself permission to be swept away by him."

Irrevocably Beautiful

Your Spirit is a jewel, truly a rare find. It's been battered also broken but is resilient and fervor. Stunning Seraphic, simply angelic, I thank God for such a Beautiful Surprise. You are a complicated beauty, one of a kind; More valuable than Triptych to me.

Your lips are succulent pears, tongue supple and divine; gracious entry into my mouth with a smooth velvet flow, orgasmic to my palate.

Your smile is captivating, mysteriously enchanting. I'm under its spell without it, I'll slowly fade. It's the fuel I need to live.

Your eyes are hypnotic, gentle and melancholic. They tantalize, criticize, empathize and mesmerize.

Your touch transcends my flesh, caressing my essence, my soul; the very defibrillation that activated the pulses of my stalled heart.

Your embrace is secure, strongly sedating, I lose all inhibitions; I'm fused to you and bound to you.

Your body, Mmm…I try to tear my gaze from, your silk, milk chocolate skin; mounds and ripples of muscle, causing spasms and yoni tension…I salivate…You intoxicate…No duplicate…I wish I could have been the hands of God so I could feel what He felt when He fashioned you. My gift…a masterpiece!

Your love is cosmic; complete and harmonious. It's spiritual, physical, incredible, exceptional…Intense! Like hurricane Katrina's flooding, like Japan's Tsunami, Oklahoma's Tornado, and Novarupta, destroying my doubts and fears. Not only shaking me but it's powerful

enough to rock those surrounding me miles deep.
Straight talk no chaser. We make fiery sunsets, wicked
midnights; I want to make your morning cock crow as you
go down the crack of my dawn.

Your love is hot like molten lava cascading down my walls,
plunging into the deep pacific forming Kilauea…Mountain
of Fire!
Molding me, creating new land; compelling me to be a
better woman

Irrevocably…you are everything…everything…Beautiful!

~Lord thank you for allowing me to see the beauty of my husband and help me to remember who he is and not what he does… Amen

Bound To You

The Lord commanded for me not to separate from you,
my husband
And commanded you not to divorce me, your wife
I will retain the place in life that the Lord assigned to me
I will remain in the situation which God has called me
I am responsible to God to remain in the situation
He called me to
That is this marriage and I'm bound to you
With marriage we will face many troubles in this life
We are concerned about the affairs of this world
How I can please you and you please me as your wife
My devotion is divided between my husband,
my lord and My Lord, My God
I will retain the place in life that the Lord assigned to me
I will remain in the situation which God has called me
I am responsible to God to remain in the situation
He has called me to that is this marriage and I'm bound to
you

~Lord, give me the grace to remain in the place where you called me. You called to me and said he is my husband, I must remain in the situation I was called. You assigned me and called me to this marriage. I am bound to my husband.
Amen

☐

I Hear You...

You mean the world to me
A treasure hidden in my heart
A perfect match for me
From the very start
The depth of your voice
The softest and tenderest of any touch
I am blessed to have a man I love
And loves me so much
I only want the best for you
For you deserve it all
And today
Relax, chill
I'm at your beckoning call

We Don't Always Get It Right…
I Apologize!

For every time I've disrespected you
For every time I didn't fully support you
For everything that I've said
That has caused your heart pain…I apologize
For every time I walked out on you
For every time I thought wrong thoughts of you
For all the time I spent being mad and not forgiving you…
I apologize
For every time that I've lied
For being full of myself and of pride
For closing off and not fully trusting you
For judging and rejecting you…I apologize
I know there's a lot more that I have done
This is me saying for all of it I was wrong
I didn't realize to what extent I've caused you such pain…
For that I apologize again and again
For every talk that turned into a fight
For being uncompromising and I just had to be right
For not handling your heart with tender care
And taking you for granted that you'll always be here…
I apologize
I hope one day I can make you smile again
And show you that I am a changing woman
I hope we can start fresh and a new
And that you can truly forgive me as I forgive you
I know that we can make it…we can make it through
I'm going to give it my all…Will you?
Our love is worth fighting for. What God has put together
no one can separate. Not even us!

~Lord give my husband clarity of thought, peace in his heart, quietness in his spirit and stillness in his soul. He has a big task guiding our family. Cover him! Just like a warm blanket, I will cover him with prayer. I'm striving to please you oh Lord, by obeying all you've asked of me concerning my husband and your man…Amen

GOD HAS DETERMINED YOUR PATH

Your path is determined by God. Walk in the steps that have been placed before you. Walk it out!

I'm not satisfied with my current position. I will let my feet do the walking. My past has held me back too long. It will no longer hold me hostage. I'm devoted to my purpose, God's will for my life. I can't go backward, I can't stay here, I must move ahead…Press forward. Even in the face of fear, I will do it afraid. I am determined about my purpose.

Stop trying to fix everything. Stop trying to figure a way to manipulate the situation. Just let things happen the way they are supposed to happen. God doesn't need help. I need to trust the process, if I really trust God, relinquish control.

God Has A Purpose

When you're down and feeling weary
When you feel you're walking alone
And you feel that all hope has gone
It's the night go ahead and cry now
But know that joy will come tomorrow
It's all part of God's own master plan

When you try to understand
And it's hard for you to stand
And it's hard to see through the tears
That blind your eyes…
That's when the Lord steps in to carry you
He promised never to leave nor forsake you
This is the path He has predestined for your life
When you're going through your storms
You're never alone
Whether it's fire or a flood
He'll keep you safe from harm
Don't be discouraged by the wind and rain
Or terror in the night
Know that God has a purpose for your life

God has a purpose
He knows the thoughts He thinks toward you
God has a purpose
He has great work assigned for you to do
We know that all things will work out for the good
According to His plan
Be still and know God has a purpose for your life

~God has given us everything pertaining to life in order to survive anything. Although things may look like they're falling apart, be of good cheer…It's not over! Things are about to get better.

Redeemed

I want to thank my Heavenly Father for all He's done for
me
He is worthy of all praise, honor and glory
I thank Him for His plan for mankind to be redeemed.
I want to thank my Christ Jesus
Our Father's begotten son
For dwelling among men coming, through 42 generations
To perform the plan of His Father
To die and set us free
Although He owned everything; yet He had nothing
Although He owned everything; yet He had nothing
I thank you Christ Jesus
You said your leaving would be profitable for me
So that I could have access to your spirit
Which would abide in me
Thank you Holy Spirit for your joy and your peace
Without you I am nothing
You're proof I've been redeemed
You've connected me to the Father
Through the death of the son
Although the three of you work separate
You are only One
Father, I thank you for your plan
Jesus, I thank you for being a man
Holy Spirit, I thank you for dwelling in me
This is proof I've been redeemed

Allow To Happen

The wind blowing a gentle breeze
Reminding me of the softness and a comforting touch
As vulnerable and fragile as a new blade of grass
My heart is full of images
Of a place where there is no time or space
Complete and utter peace
HOTEP…mind consumed visions of you
Abstract art a complicated masterpiece
That only the chosen can comprehend
The true message behind the artist's hand
Folded inside out
Exposing the inner most
The gutter most part of who we are
Our soul…

Hand to man
Heart to God there is nothing left to figure out
One with the earth that brought you out
And now standing at the ocean door
As far as the eye can see
Nothing but a blue heaven
That I can reach out and touch with my hand
I can tread upon and be cleansed
Of all doubt ever knowing
And fear of showing and being who I am

A flower knows when to bloom
A bird knows when to sing
The clouds know when to give rain

And all things know when to grow
Why complicate it...
Just allow it to happen

~Don't forget that after every storm there is growth. Every situation in life has been allowed in order that you grow. Don't fight the process, you'll only prolong it. Embrace It!

Consider the heavens, the billions of galaxies; the stars are the breath of God's mouth. God is mighty, He is strong. He has the strength to see you through...Just trust Him!

Every situation in life has been allowed in order that you grow. Don't fight the process, you'll only prolong it.

FAITH'S PROTECTION

Fight the good fight of faith. Faith is the substance of things hoped for the evidence of things not seen. Belief is the energy that causes atoms to come together to manifest in the form of matter the thing that is desired. Belief brings into existence whatever you undoubtedly believe in. This includes good and bad…What have you believed? Believe God's Word…No doubt, only believe. Don't fill your mind with doubt. Now understand the importance of these pieces of the armor of God.

The shield of faith and the sword of the spirit are in your hands. You believe in whatever you hold on to. Your belief is in the Word of God…and His Word only. Keep your hands on your weapons and don't let go. Arm yourself.

Most of what we have believed in times past is what others have said; not what God has said. We have armor on but it's not of God, it's of the enemy. It's fake and non-effective; basically, a costume. We are holding onto his lies which become matter in our lives. Always attacking the truth; enslaving us and holding us captive by all the lies. The shield of faith protects our most intimate place. Truth is hidden in our loins. This is where things are birthed. God gave us all the measure of faith. We all have the energy to produce matter from the truth of God's Word and from the lies of Satan. This is why Satan is called the father of lies. We didn't use the proper protection and we were impregnated by him, the liar, and all he can produce are lies. Shield your truth – God's truth concerning you and produce matter that is good. The Holy Spirit will guide you into all truth. Follow the way. Believe the truth. Produce life.

Lord you are the life giver and Satan is the lie giver. Whatever lies I have become impregnated with I reject and abort them. The truth of your word will cause and bring forth life and not lies. Help me to always include the "F" in any lie. Father you are the "F". You make the difference.

Life without the "F" is lie. You need the "F" which is our Father in heaven included in your life. He is the Life giver and satan is a lie giver and the father of all lies.

~Lord, Help me to hold onto my shield of faith and your word daily. I must pick them up, grab them and hold on to them for dear life. My life depends on them. It really does matter. Faith is an expression of God's grace. It is a gift. Use it skillfully and wisely. Amen

Branded Jesus

Branded Jesus, how great you are
You are raised, lifted up and highly exalted
For the glorious work you've done
You hung, bled and died...On Golgotha crucified
You were unloved and unwanted by men
Yet you died and called us your friend
A man of sadness, familiar with suffering
You weren't considered to be worth nothing
No beauty...No splendor...Unenviable
You were punished for our wrongdoing
The iniquity of us all
Took our suffering, carried our regrets
Redeemed us by your bloodshed upon the cross
Branded Jesus...Healer You Are

~ Lord, help me do as you've instructed. Show me what actions to take when there is a need for a physical demonstration of love and support. Give me the wisdom that I need in order to encourage with words to comfort when it's needed or if anything is needed to be done at all. Amen

~God is not concerned about what I think; only what He has said for me to do. He will equip me to do what He has chosen me to do. God will not patronize me. His assignment supersedes my plans. No matter how great my plans are or who I think it will bless. God knows best!

"No matter where you go or how far away you are; you are never too far for the hand of God to reach you."

I Want To Be Free...

I want to be free, I want to be free
Any place, where I go, I want my mind to be at ease
I want to be free, so free
With my head raised to the sky
Spread my wings so I can fly and be free
Free as the wind blowing, a butterfly taking flight
A stream of water finding its way out to the sea
A bumble bee flying in springtime
And wildflowers taken bloom
Like a new born baby fighting its way out the womb
I want to be free, so free, to be the one I was destined to
be
Coming out of the old mentality
No longer rehearsing lines for their skit
It's time for me to live for me…I want to be free
I want to be free
Any place, where I go, I want my mind to be at ease
I want to be free, so free
With my head raised to the sky, spread my wings
So I can fly and be free
Free as the wind blowing, a butterfly taking flight
Looking back on yesterday, wondering how did I get this
way
Trapped in a real life TV show
I know the life I've had the pain and suffering
I can't repeat the past
Constantly lying to myself a dreadful thing to do
But now it's time…To my own self be true
My eyes are wide open, my heart is fixed

No more playing games, no more deceiving tricks
Falling free like the rain, refreshing the earth
Showering seeds of the universal womb
Taking time from the hustle and bustle, to be silent
And with myself commune
Here we know there's karma
The choice maker and our purpose in life
Relying on the Spirit within, The Creator of all life
He created you, for you to be a gift to humanity
Not trying to be like anyone but me
How liberating it is to be not consumed
With pleasing man and all they presume
I'm going to live my life, just like the air I breathe
In and out my lungs it flows totally free

"No matter what I planned in my heart. God has shown me that He has determined my every step…just follow HIM, TRUST HIM!"

Purple Butterfly

Purple butterfly
You are beautiful
More precious than ever
You are resilient, a survivor
With life comes ups and downs
Sometimes you laugh and wear a smile
Through the pain and rain clouds
Stand strong and refuse to be knocked down
Freely fly your course
Purple butterfly

Look At Me!

Climbing insurmountable mountains
people said I couldn't climb
Exceeding beyond my own expectations
Even I said I couldn't do it
Look at me
How did I get here
I can't remember the way
All I ever wanted
Was to live a normal life one day
Look at me
It must be a dream
Please don't wake me now
I want to remember how I got here
There must be a way somehow
Now the path that I'm on
Where will it lead me
From the bottom to the top
I hope not back on bottom
It will be a devastating drop
Look at me
Plain ol' me
Making something out of life
I held myself down so long
Not knowing I could stand on my own
So dependent and helpless I was
Never thinking I could rise above
That gutter that I was lying in
Full of sorrow and grief
Dead women and men

Look at me
I can't believe my eyes
The accomplishments came without lies
No deceit just plain ol' me
I realize now how valuable for me I could be

How did I get to where I am
Climbing insurmountable mountains
People said I couldn't climb
Exceeding beyond my own expectations
Even I said I couldn't do it
But I did
Look at me

~ No one else could do the thing you've done
You gave me renewed life…a purpose driven one
My life I no longer live for me, but rather You living in
and out through me

ABOUT THE AUTHOR

Kimberly Elizabeth Maddox-Beasley a native of Detroit, Michigan is the youngest of four siblings. She is happily married to the love of her life and best friend. She and her husband of 15 years share 2 sons. Kimberly and her husband relocated to the great state of Texas in 2004 where they currently reside. She attended Texas Woman's University where she majored in Social Work.

In 2011 Kimberly had to learn to live life in a completely different manner after being diagnosed with the chronic autoimmune disease Polymyositis and later discovered that it was overlapped Lupus. As if that wasn't enough, also in 2013 she was diagnosed with an extremely rare cancer. To date I am happy to say her Lupus is controlled and her cancer is in remission.

Kimberly is a traditional woman with steadfast faith in God. She attributes her overcoming ability to her faith in God and the love and support from her family.

As a young girl, Kimberly loved writing letters and poetry to her parents. It was oftentimes their gift for birthdays and anniversaries. She has always had a love for writing.

To her writing is an oasis that she can visit at any time.